50 Sweet and Savory Recipes

By: Kelly Johnson

Table of Contents

- Thai Spring Rolls (Poh Pia)
- Thai Fried Bananas (Kluai Tod)
- Thai Coconut Pancakes (Khanom Krok)
- Thai Fish Cakes (Tod Mun Pla)
- Spicy Thai Peanuts
- Thai Rice Crackers
- Thai Sticky Rice with Mango (Khao Niew Mamuang)
- Thai Corn Fritters
- Thai Sesame Balls (Bua Loy)
- Thai Fried Tofu Bites
- Thai Sweet Potato Balls
- Thai Grilled Chicken Skewers (Gai Yang)
- Thai Coconut Macaroons
- Thai Sweet and Savory Coconut Rolls (Khanom Pang Sangkhaya)
- Thai Chili Lime Edamame
- Thai Tofu Satay
- Thai Cucumber Salad with Peanuts
- Thai Mango Salad
- Thai Coconut Custard (Sangkaya)
- Thai Grilled Corn with Coconut Cream
- Thai Rice Flour Cakes
- Thai Eggplant Chips
- Thai Vegetable Samosas
- Thai Savory Coconut Rice Balls
- Thai Sweet Corn Pudding (Kanom Khao Pod)
- Thai Spicy Cashew Nuts
- Thai Fried Sweet Potato Chips
- Thai Coconut and Taro Dessert
- Thai Avocado Salad
- Thai Hot and Sour Soup (Tom Yum)
- Thai Banana in Coconut Milk (Kluai Buat Chi)
- Thai Sweet Sticky Rice with Taro (Khao Niew Mamuang)
- Thai Chive Dumplings
- Thai Coconut and Pandan Jelly
- Thai Green Mango Salad with Fish Sauce

- Thai Savory Pancakes (Khanom Bueang)
- Thai Coconut Cream Custard (Khanom Kathi)
- Thai Chili and Garlic Potato Wedges
- Thai Grilled Eggplant Salad (Yam Makheua Yao)
- Thai Sweet and Spicy Cucumber Pickles
- Thai Almond Tofu Dessert
- Thai Watermelon Salad
- Thai Chili Lime Popcorn
- Thai Savory Mung Bean Pancakes
- Thai Sweet Sticky Rice with Black Sesame
- Thai Fish Ball Soup
- Thai Sesame Chicken Wings
- Thai Curry Puffs
- Thai Fried Wontons
- Thai Sweet Potato and Coconut Dessert

Thai Spring Rolls (Poh Pia)

Ingredients:

- 10 spring roll wrappers
- 1 cup shredded cabbage
- 1 cup shredded carrots
- 1/2 cup bean sprouts
- 1/4 cup mushrooms, sliced
- 2 cloves garlic, minced
- 2 tablespoons soy sauce
- Oil for frying

Instructions:

1. **Prepare Filling:**
    - In a skillet, sauté garlic until fragrant. Add cabbage, carrots, mushrooms, and bean sprouts. Stir-fry for 3-4 minutes and add soy sauce. Remove from heat.
2. **Wrap Spring Rolls:**
    - Place a spring roll wrapper on a clean surface. Add a spoonful of the filling and fold the sides over. Roll tightly to seal.
3. **Fry:**
    - Heat oil in a pan over medium heat. Fry spring rolls until golden brown on all sides. Drain on paper towels.
4. **Serve:**
    - Serve with sweet chili sauce for dipping.

Thai Fried Bananas (Kluai Tod)

Ingredients:

- 4 ripe bananas, sliced
- 1 cup all-purpose flour
- 1/2 cup rice flour
- 1/4 cup sugar
- 1/2 cup coconut milk
- Oil for frying

Instructions:

1. **Make Batter:**
   - In a bowl, mix flour, rice flour, sugar, and coconut milk until smooth.
2. **Fry Bananas:**
   - Heat oil in a pan. Dip banana slices into the batter and carefully place them in the hot oil. Fry until golden brown.
3. **Drain:**
   - Remove and drain on paper towels.
4. **Serve:**
   - Serve warm, optionally dusted with powdered sugar.

Thai Coconut Pancakes (Khanom Krok)

Ingredients:

- 1 cup rice flour
- 1 cup coconut milk
- 1/2 cup water
- 1/4 cup sugar
- 1/2 teaspoon salt
- Chopped green onions for topping

Instructions:

1. **Make Batter:**
    - In a bowl, mix rice flour, coconut milk, water, sugar, and salt until smooth.
2. **Cook:**
    - Preheat a pancake pan or mold. Pour a spoonful of the batter into each mold and cook until the edges begin to set.
3. **Add Toppings:**
    - Sprinkle chopped green onions on top and cover until cooked through.
4. **Serve:**
    - Serve warm as a snack.

Thai Fish Cakes (Tod Mun Pla)

Ingredients:

- 1 pound fish fillets, minced
- 1 tablespoon red curry paste
- 1/2 cup green beans, finely chopped
- 1 egg
- 1 tablespoon fish sauce
- Oil for frying

Instructions:

1. **Make Mixture:**
    - In a bowl, combine minced fish, red curry paste, egg, fish sauce, and green beans. Mix until well combined.
2. **Shape Cakes:**
    - Shape the mixture into small patties.
3. **Fry:**
    - Heat oil in a pan. Fry the fish cakes until golden brown on both sides.
4. **Serve:**
    - Serve with sweet chili sauce.

Spicy Thai Peanuts

Ingredients:

- 2 cups raw peanuts
- 1 tablespoon vegetable oil
- 1 tablespoon sugar
- 1 teaspoon chili powder
- 1/2 teaspoon salt

Instructions:

1. **Prepare Peanuts:**
    - In a skillet, heat oil over medium heat. Add peanuts and cook for 5-7 minutes until golden.
2. **Season:**
    - Stir in sugar, chili powder, and salt. Cook for an additional 2 minutes.
3. **Cool:**
    - Remove from heat and let cool.
4. **Serve:**
    - Serve as a snack or appetizer.

Thai Rice Crackers

Ingredients:

- 1 cup rice flour
- 1/2 cup water
- 1/2 teaspoon salt
- Oil for frying

Instructions:

1. **Make Dough:**
   - In a bowl, mix rice flour, water, and salt until a smooth dough forms.
2. **Shape Crackers:**
   - Take small portions of dough and flatten them into thin discs.
3. **Fry:**
   - Heat oil in a pan. Fry the discs until crispy and golden brown.
4. **Serve:**
   - Serve as a snack or with dips.

Thai Sticky Rice with Mango (Khao Niew Mamuang)

Ingredients:

- 1 cup sticky rice
- 1 can (400 ml) coconut milk
- 1/2 cup sugar
- 1/4 teaspoon salt
- 2 ripe mangoes, sliced

Instructions:

1. **Prepare Rice:**
    - Soak sticky rice in water for at least 4 hours. Steam until cooked.
2. **Make Coconut Sauce:**
    - In a saucepan, heat coconut milk, sugar, and salt until dissolved.
3. **Combine:**
    - Mix a portion of the coconut sauce with the cooked sticky rice.
4. **Serve:**
    - Serve sticky rice topped with mango slices and drizzle with remaining coconut sauce.

Thai Corn Fritters

Ingredients:

- 1 cup corn kernels
- 1/2 cup all-purpose flour
- 1/4 cup coconut milk
- 1/4 cup chopped green onions
- 1/2 teaspoon salt
- Oil for frying

Instructions:

1. **Make Batter:**
    - In a bowl, combine corn, flour, coconut milk, green onions, and salt.
2. **Fry Fritters:**
    - Heat oil in a pan. Drop spoonfuls of batter into the hot oil and fry until golden brown.
3. **Drain:**
    - Remove and drain on paper towels.
4. **Serve:**
    - Serve warm with sweet chili sauce.

Thai Sesame Balls (Bua Loy)

Ingredients:

- 1 cup glutinous rice flour
- 1/4 cup water
- 1/4 cup sesame seeds
- 1 cup coconut milk
- 1/4 cup sugar
- 1/4 teaspoon salt

Instructions:

1. **Make Dough:**
    - In a bowl, mix glutinous rice flour and water until a smooth dough forms.
2. **Shape Balls:**
    - Roll the dough into small balls and coat with sesame seeds.
3. **Fry:**
    - Heat oil in a pan. Fry the balls until golden brown and float to the surface.
4. **Make Sauce:**
    - In a saucepan, heat coconut milk, sugar, and salt until dissolved.
5. **Serve:**
    - Serve sesame balls drizzled with sweet coconut sauce.

Thai Fried Tofu Bites

Ingredients:

- 1 block firm tofu, drained and pressed
- 1/2 cup cornstarch
- Oil for frying
- Soy sauce for dipping

Instructions:

1. **Prepare Tofu:**
   - Cut tofu into bite-sized cubes.
2. **Coat Tofu:**
   - Dredge tofu cubes in cornstarch until fully coated.
3. **Fry:**
   - Heat oil in a pan over medium heat. Fry tofu until golden brown on all sides. Drain on paper towels.
4. **Serve:**
   - Serve with soy sauce for dipping.

Thai Sweet Potato Balls

Ingredients:

- 1 cup sweet potatoes, cooked and mashed
- 1/2 cup rice flour
- 1/4 cup sugar
- Oil for frying
- Sesame seeds for coating

Instructions:

1. **Make Mixture:**
   - In a bowl, mix mashed sweet potatoes, rice flour, and sugar until combined.
2. **Shape Balls:**
   - Roll mixture into small balls and coat with sesame seeds.
3. **Fry:**
   - Heat oil in a pan. Fry balls until golden brown.
4. **Serve:**
   - Serve warm as a snack.

Thai Grilled Chicken Skewers (Gai Yang)

Ingredients:

- 1 pound chicken thighs, cut into pieces
- 2 tablespoons soy sauce
- 1 tablespoon fish sauce
- 1 tablespoon sugar
- 1 tablespoon garlic, minced
- Skewers

Instructions:

1. **Marinate Chicken:**
    - In a bowl, mix soy sauce, fish sauce, sugar, and garlic. Add chicken and marinate for at least 30 minutes.
2. **Skewer:**
    - Thread marinated chicken onto skewers.
3. **Grill:**
    - Grill skewers over medium heat until cooked through and slightly charred.
4. **Serve:**
    - Serve with a dipping sauce.

Thai Coconut Macaroons

Ingredients:

- 2 cups shredded coconut
- 1/2 cup sweetened condensed milk
- 1 teaspoon vanilla extract
- 2 egg whites
- A pinch of salt

Instructions:

1. **Preheat Oven:**
   - Preheat oven to 325°F (160°C).
2. **Mix Ingredients:**
   - In a bowl, combine coconut, condensed milk, vanilla, egg whites, and salt.
3. **Shape Cookies:**
   - Drop spoonfuls of the mixture onto a baking sheet.
4. **Bake:**
   - Bake for 15-20 minutes until golden brown.
5. **Serve:**
   - Let cool before serving.

Thai Sweet and Savory Coconut Rolls (Khanom Pang Sangkhaya)

Ingredients:

- 1 cup all-purpose flour
- 1 cup coconut milk
- 1/2 cup sugar
- 1/2 teaspoon salt
- Banana leaves or parchment paper

Instructions:

1. **Prepare Batter:**
   - In a bowl, mix flour, coconut milk, sugar, and salt until smooth.
2. **Wrap:**
   - Pour batter into banana leaves or parchment paper, folding to create a small packet.
3. **Steam:**
   - Steam packets for 20-30 minutes until cooked through.
4. **Serve:**
   - Serve warm or at room temperature.

Thai Chili Lime Edamame

Ingredients:

- 2 cups edamame (in pods)
- 1 tablespoon olive oil
- 1 teaspoon chili powder
- Zest and juice of 1 lime
- Salt to taste

Instructions:

1. **Cook Edamame:**
   - Boil edamame in salted water for 5-7 minutes until tender. Drain.
2. **Season:**
   - In a bowl, toss edamame with olive oil, chili powder, lime zest, lime juice, and salt.
3. **Serve:**
   - Serve warm as an appetizer or snack.

Thai Tofu Satay

Ingredients:

- 1 block firm tofu, drained and pressed
- 2 tablespoons soy sauce
- 1 tablespoon curry powder
- 1 tablespoon coconut milk
- Skewers
- Peanut sauce for serving

Instructions:

1. **Prepare Tofu:**
    - Cut tofu into strips.
2. **Marinate Tofu:**
    - In a bowl, mix soy sauce, curry powder, and coconut milk. Marinate tofu for 30 minutes.
3. **Skewer:**
    - Thread marinated tofu onto skewers.
4. **Grill:**
    - Grill skewers until heated through and slightly charred.
5. **Serve:**
    - Serve with peanut sauce.

Thai Cucumber Salad with Peanuts

Ingredients:

- 2 cucumbers, thinly sliced
- 1/2 cup roasted peanuts, crushed
- 1 tablespoon sugar
- 2 tablespoons rice vinegar
- 1 tablespoon fish sauce
- Fresh cilantro for garnish

Instructions:

1. **Make Dressing:**
   - In a bowl, whisk together sugar, rice vinegar, and fish sauce until sugar dissolves.
2. **Combine:**
   - In a salad bowl, combine cucumbers, peanuts, and dressing. Toss to coat.
3. **Garnish:**
   - Garnish with fresh cilantro.
4. **Serve:**
   - Serve chilled or at room temperature.

Thai Mango Salad

Ingredients:

- 2 ripe mangoes, julienned
- 1 bell pepper, sliced
- 1 carrot, shredded
- 1/4 cup fresh cilantro, chopped
- 1/4 cup peanuts, crushed
- 2 tablespoons lime juice
- 1 tablespoon fish sauce
- 1 tablespoon sugar

Instructions:

1. **Make Dressing:**
   - In a bowl, whisk together lime juice, fish sauce, and sugar.
2. **Combine Salad:**
   - In a salad bowl, combine mangoes, bell pepper, carrot, cilantro, and peanuts.
3. **Dress Salad:**
   - Pour dressing over the salad and toss gently to combine.
4. **Serve:**
   - Serve immediately as a refreshing side dish.

Thai Coconut Custard (Sangkaya)

Ingredients:

- 1 cup coconut milk
- 1/2 cup sugar
- 4 large eggs
- 1/2 teaspoon salt
- 1 tablespoon pandan juice (optional)

Instructions:

1. **Preheat Oven:**
   - Preheat oven to 350°F (175°C).
2. **Mix Ingredients:**
   - In a bowl, whisk together coconut milk, sugar, eggs, salt, and pandan juice until smooth.
3. **Prepare Baking Dish:**
   - Pour the mixture into a greased baking dish.
4. **Bake:**
   - Bake in a water bath for 30-40 minutes until set.
5. **Cool and Serve:**
   - Let cool before slicing and serving.

Thai Grilled Corn with Coconut Cream

Ingredients:

- 4 ears of corn, husked
- 1 cup coconut milk
- 1 tablespoon sugar
- A pinch of salt
- 1 tablespoon coconut flakes (for garnish)

Instructions:

1. **Grill Corn:**
   - Grill corn over medium heat, turning occasionally, until charred and tender.
2. **Prepare Coconut Cream:**
   - In a saucepan, combine coconut milk, sugar, and salt. Heat until sugar dissolves.
3. **Serve:**
   - Brush grilled corn with coconut cream and sprinkle with coconut flakes before serving.

Thai Rice Flour Cakes

Ingredients:

- 1 cup rice flour
- 1/2 cup coconut milk
- 1/4 cup sugar
- A pinch of salt
- Banana leaves or small cups for steaming

Instructions:

1. **Prepare Mixture:**
   - In a bowl, mix rice flour, coconut milk, sugar, and salt until smooth.
2. **Fill Molds:**
   - Pour mixture into banana leaves or small cups.
3. **Steam:**
   - Steam for 20-30 minutes until cooked through.
4. **Serve:**
   - Let cool slightly before serving.

Thai Eggplant Chips

Ingredients:

- 2 Thai eggplants, thinly sliced
- 1/4 cup rice flour
- Oil for frying
- Salt to taste

Instructions:

1. **Coat Eggplants:**
    - Toss eggplant slices in rice flour until coated.
2. **Fry:**
    - Heat oil in a pan and fry eggplant slices until golden and crispy. Drain on paper towels.
3. **Serve:**
    - Sprinkle with salt and serve as a snack.

Thai Vegetable Samosas

Ingredients:

- 1 cup all-purpose flour
- 1/4 cup water
- 2 tablespoons oil
- 1 cup mixed vegetables (peas, carrots, potatoes)
- 1 teaspoon curry powder
- Oil for frying

Instructions:

1. **Make Dough:**
    - Mix flour, water, and oil to form a dough. Rest for 30 minutes.
2. **Prepare Filling:**
    - Cook mixed vegetables with curry powder until tender. Let cool.
3. **Shape Samosas:**
    - Roll out dough, cut into circles, and fill with vegetable mixture. Fold and seal.
4. **Fry:**
    - Heat oil in a pan and fry samosas until golden brown.
5. **Serve:**
    - Serve with chutney or dipping sauce.

Thai Savory Coconut Rice Balls

Ingredients:

- 1 cup glutinous rice, soaked overnight
- 1/2 cup coconut milk
- 1/4 teaspoon salt
- Sesame seeds for coating

Instructions:

1. **Prepare Rice:**
    - Drain and rinse soaked rice. Steam until cooked.
2. **Mix Coconut:**
    - In a bowl, mix cooked rice with coconut milk and salt.
3. **Shape Balls:**
    - Shape the mixture into small balls and roll in sesame seeds.
4. **Serve:**
    - Serve warm or at room temperature.

Thai Sweet Corn Pudding (Kanom Khao Pod)

Ingredients:

- 1 cup fresh corn kernels
- 1/2 cup coconut milk
- 1/4 cup rice flour
- 1/4 cup sugar
- A pinch of salt

Instructions:

1. **Prepare Mixture:**
    - In a blender, combine corn, coconut milk, rice flour, sugar, and salt until smooth.
2. **Pour into Molds:**
    - Pour mixture into small cups or molds.
3. **Steam:**
    - Steam for 20-25 minutes until set.
4. **Serve:**
    - Let cool before serving.

Thai Spicy Cashew Nuts

Ingredients:

- 2 cups raw cashew nuts
- 1 tablespoon vegetable oil
- 1 tablespoon chili powder
- 1 tablespoon sugar
- Salt to taste

Instructions:

1. **Toast Cashews:**
   - Heat oil in a pan and add cashew nuts. Toast until golden brown.
2. **Season:**
   - Remove from heat and mix in chili powder, sugar, and salt while still warm.
3. **Serve:**
   - Let cool and serve as a spicy snack.

Thai Fried Sweet Potato Chips

Ingredients:

- 2 large sweet potatoes, thinly sliced
- Oil for frying
- Salt to taste

Instructions:

1. **Prepare Oil:**
   - Heat oil in a deep frying pan over medium heat.
2. **Fry Sweet Potatoes:**
   - Fry the sweet potato slices in batches until golden and crispy. Remove and drain on paper towels.
3. **Season:**
   - Sprinkle with salt while still warm.
4. **Serve:**
   - Enjoy as a snack or appetizer.

Thai Coconut and Taro Dessert

Ingredients:

- 1 cup taro, peeled and diced
- 1 cup coconut milk
- 1/2 cup sugar
- 1/4 cup rice flour
- A pinch of salt

Instructions:

1. **Cook Taro:**
    - Steam or boil diced taro until tender.
2. **Make Mixture:**
    - In a bowl, mix cooked taro with coconut milk, sugar, rice flour, and salt until smooth.
3. **Steam:**
    - Pour the mixture into a greased dish and steam for about 30 minutes until set.
4. **Serve:**
    - Allow to cool before cutting into squares.

Thai Avocado Salad

Ingredients:

- 2 ripe avocados, diced
- 1 cup cherry tomatoes, halved
- 1/4 cup red onion, thinly sliced
- 1/4 cup fresh cilantro, chopped
- Juice of 1 lime
- Salt and pepper to taste

Instructions:

1. **Combine Ingredients:**
    - In a bowl, mix avocados, cherry tomatoes, red onion, and cilantro.
2. **Dress Salad:**
    - Drizzle lime juice over the salad and season with salt and pepper.
3. **Serve:**
    - Serve immediately as a refreshing side dish.

Thai Hot and Sour Soup (Tom Yum)

Ingredients:

- 4 cups chicken or vegetable broth
- 2 stalks lemongrass, smashed
- 3-4 kaffir lime leaves
- 200g shrimp, peeled and deveined
- 200g mushrooms, sliced
- 2-3 Thai bird chilies, smashed
- 2 tablespoons fish sauce
- Juice of 1 lime
- Fresh cilantro for garnish

Instructions:

1. **Prepare Broth:**
   - In a pot, bring the broth to a boil. Add lemongrass and kaffir lime leaves.
2. **Add Shrimp and Mushrooms:**
   - Add shrimp and mushrooms, cooking until shrimp turns pink.
3. **Season Soup:**
   - Stir in bird chilies, fish sauce, and lime juice. Adjust seasoning to taste.
4. **Serve:**
   - Garnish with cilantro before serving.

Thai Banana in Coconut Milk (Kluai Buat Chi)

Ingredients:

- 4 ripe bananas, sliced
- 1 cup coconut milk
- 1/2 cup sugar
- A pinch of salt

Instructions:

1. **Cook Coconut Milk:**
   - In a saucepan, combine coconut milk, sugar, and salt. Heat until dissolved.
2. **Add Bananas:**
   - Add sliced bananas to the coconut mixture and simmer for a few minutes until tender.
3. **Serve:**
   - Let cool slightly and serve warm or chilled.

Thai Sweet Sticky Rice with Taro (Khao Niew Mamuang)

Ingredients:

- 1 cup glutinous rice, soaked overnight
- 1/2 cup coconut milk
- 1/4 cup sugar
- 1/2 cup taro, peeled and diced
- A pinch of salt

Instructions:

1. **Prepare Rice:**
   - Drain and rinse the soaked rice. Steam the rice until cooked.
2. **Cook Taro:**
   - Steam diced taro until tender.
3. **Mix Coconut:**
   - In a saucepan, combine coconut milk, sugar, and salt. Heat until sugar dissolves.
4. **Combine:**
   - Mix cooked rice with half of the coconut milk mixture. Serve with taro and remaining coconut milk.

Thai Chive Dumplings

Ingredients:

- 1 cup rice flour
- 1/2 cup water
- 1 cup chives, chopped
- 1/2 teaspoon salt
- Oil for frying

Instructions:

1. **Make Dough:**
    - Combine rice flour, water, and salt to form a dough. Mix in chopped chives.
2. **Shape Dumplings:**
    - Form small patties or dumplings with the mixture.
3. **Fry:**
    - Heat oil in a pan and fry dumplings until golden brown on both sides.
4. **Serve:**
    - Serve with soy sauce or chili sauce for dipping.

Thai Coconut and Pandan Jelly

Ingredients:

- 1 cup coconut milk
- 1 cup pandan juice (or pandan extract)
- 1/2 cup sugar
- 2 tablespoons agar-agar powder

Instructions:

1. **Mix Ingredients:**
   - In a saucepan, combine coconut milk, pandan juice, sugar, and agar-agar. Stir well.
2. **Heat Mixture:**
   - Bring to a boil, stirring continuously until agar-agar dissolves.
3. **Set Jelly:**
   - Pour the mixture into a mold and let cool until set.
4. **Serve:**
   - Cut into cubes and serve chilled.

Thai Green Mango Salad with Fish Sauce

Ingredients:

- 2 green mangoes, julienned
- 1 carrot, julienned
- 1/4 cup red onion, thinly sliced
- 1/4 cup fresh cilantro, chopped
- 2 tablespoons fish sauce
- 1 tablespoon lime juice
- 1 tablespoon sugar
- 1-2 Thai bird chilies, finely chopped (optional)

Instructions:

1. **Combine Ingredients:**
   - In a large bowl, mix the green mango, carrot, red onion, and cilantro.
2. **Make Dressing:**
   - In a small bowl, whisk together fish sauce, lime juice, sugar, and chilies.
3. **Toss Salad:**
   - Pour the dressing over the salad and toss to combine.
4. **Serve:**
   - Serve immediately as a refreshing side dish.

Thai Savory Pancakes (Khanom Bueang)

Ingredients:

- 1 cup rice flour
- 1/2 cup water
- 1/4 cup coconut milk
- 1/2 teaspoon salt
- 1/4 cup mung bean, cooked
- 1/4 cup shredded coconut
- 1 tablespoon sugar

Instructions:

1. **Prepare Batter:**
    - In a bowl, mix rice flour, water, coconut milk, and salt until smooth.
2. **Cook Pancakes:**
    - Heat a non-stick pan over medium heat. Pour a small amount of batter, spreading it thinly. Sprinkle mung bean and shredded coconut on top. Cook until the edges turn golden.
3. **Fold:**
    - Fold the pancake in half and cook for an additional minute.
4. **Serve:**
    - Serve warm with a sprinkle of sugar.

Thai Coconut Cream Custard (Khanom Kathi)

Ingredients:

- 1 cup coconut milk
- 1/2 cup rice flour
- 1/4 cup sugar
- A pinch of salt
- 1/2 teaspoon pandan extract (optional)

Instructions:

1. **Mix Ingredients:**
   - In a bowl, combine coconut milk, rice flour, sugar, salt, and pandan extract. Whisk until smooth.
2. **Steam Custard:**
   - Pour the mixture into small cups. Steam for about 30 minutes until set.
3. **Cool:**
   - Allow to cool before serving.
4. **Serve:**
   - Serve chilled or at room temperature.

Thai Chili and Garlic Potato Wedges

Ingredients:

- 4 medium potatoes, cut into wedges
- 2 tablespoons oil
- 3 cloves garlic, minced
- 1-2 Thai bird chilies, chopped
- Salt to taste
- Fresh cilantro for garnish

Instructions:

1. **Prepare Potatoes:**
    - Preheat the oven to 425°F (220°C). Toss potato wedges with oil, garlic, chilies, and salt.
2. **Bake:**
    - Spread the wedges on a baking sheet and bake for 25-30 minutes until golden brown and crispy.
3. **Garnish:**
    - Sprinkle with fresh cilantro before serving.
4. **Serve:**
    - Serve hot as a snack or side dish.

Thai Grilled Eggplant Salad (Yam Makheua Yao)

Ingredients:

- 2 large eggplants
- 1/4 cup red onion, thinly sliced
- 1/4 cup fresh cilantro, chopped
- 2 tablespoons fish sauce
- 1 tablespoon lime juice
- 1 tablespoon sugar
- 1-2 Thai bird chilies, finely chopped (optional)

Instructions:

1. **Grill Eggplants:**
   - Grill eggplants over medium heat until charred and tender. Let cool and slice.
2. **Combine Ingredients:**
   - In a bowl, combine grilled eggplant, red onion, cilantro, fish sauce, lime juice, sugar, and chilies.
3. **Toss Salad:**
   - Toss to combine and adjust seasoning to taste.
4. **Serve:**
   - Serve warm or at room temperature.

Thai Sweet and Spicy Cucumber Pickles

Ingredients:

- 2 cucumbers, thinly sliced
- 1/2 cup sugar
- 1/2 cup vinegar
- 1/4 cup water
- 1-2 Thai bird chilies, sliced
- A pinch of salt

Instructions:

1. **Make Pickling Liquid:**
    - In a saucepan, combine sugar, vinegar, water, chilies, and salt. Heat until sugar dissolves.
2. **Combine Cucumbers:**
    - Place cucumber slices in a jar and pour the pickling liquid over them.
3. **Pickle:**
    - Let sit for at least 30 minutes before serving.
4. **Serve:**
    - Serve as a tangy side dish.

Thai Almond Tofu Dessert

Ingredients:

- 1/2 cup almond milk
- 1 tablespoon agar-agar powder
- 1/4 cup sugar
- 1 teaspoon vanilla extract
- Fresh fruits for topping

Instructions:

1. **Combine Ingredients:**
   - In a saucepan, combine almond milk, agar-agar, sugar, and vanilla. Stir until mixed.
2. **Heat Mixture:**
   - Bring to a boil, stirring constantly. Simmer for 2 minutes until agar-agar dissolves.
3. **Set Tofu:**
   - Pour into a mold and let cool until set.
4. **Serve:**
   - Cut into cubes and serve with fresh fruits.

Thai Watermelon Salad

Ingredients:

- 4 cups watermelon, cubed
- 1/4 cup red onion, thinly sliced
- 1/4 cup fresh mint, chopped
- Juice of 1 lime
- Salt to taste
- 1-2 Thai bird chilies, sliced (optional)

Instructions:

1. **Combine Ingredients:**
    - In a large bowl, mix watermelon, red onion, mint, lime juice, salt, and chilies.
2. **Toss Salad:**
    - Toss gently to combine.
3. **Serve:**
    - Serve immediately as a refreshing salad.

Thai Chili Lime Popcorn

Ingredients:

- 1/2 cup popcorn kernels
- 2 tablespoons vegetable oil
- Zest and juice of 1 lime
- 1 teaspoon chili powder
- Salt to taste

Instructions:

1. **Pop Popcorn:**
    - In a large pot, heat oil over medium heat. Add popcorn kernels and cover. Once popping slows, remove from heat.
2. **Season:**
    - In a bowl, mix lime zest, lime juice, chili powder, and salt. Pour over popcorn and toss to coat.
3. **Serve:**
    - Serve immediately as a spicy snack.

Thai Savory Mung Bean Pancakes

Ingredients:

- 1 cup mung bean flour
- 1/2 cup water
- 1/4 cup green onions, chopped
- 1/4 cup cilantro, chopped
- Salt to taste
- Oil for frying

Instructions:

1. **Prepare Batter:**
    - In a bowl, mix mung bean flour, water, green onions, cilantro, and salt until smooth.
2. **Cook Pancakes:**
    - Heat oil in a non-stick pan over medium heat. Pour in batter to form pancakes and cook until golden on both sides.
3. **Serve:**
    - Serve warm with dipping sauce.

Thai Sweet Sticky Rice with Black Sesame

Ingredients:

- 1 cup glutinous rice
- 1 cup coconut milk
- 1/4 cup sugar
- 1/4 teaspoon salt
- 2 tablespoons black sesame seeds

Instructions:

1. **Soak Rice:**
    - Soak glutinous rice in water for at least 4 hours or overnight.
2. **Steam Rice:**
    - Drain and steam rice for about 20 minutes until cooked.
3. **Combine Ingredients:**
    - In a saucepan, heat coconut milk, sugar, and salt until dissolved. Stir in black sesame seeds.
4. **Mix:**
    - Pour the coconut mixture over the cooked rice and let it sit for 10 minutes before serving.

Thai Fish Ball Soup

Ingredients:

- 300g fish balls
- 4 cups chicken or vegetable broth
- 1 cup bok choy, chopped
- 1/2 cup mushrooms, sliced
- 2 tablespoons soy sauce
- 1 tablespoon fish sauce
- Fresh cilantro for garnish

Instructions:

1. **Heat Broth:**
    - In a pot, bring the broth to a simmer.
2. **Add Ingredients:**
    - Add fish balls, bok choy, and mushrooms. Cook for about 5-7 minutes until heated through.
3. **Season:**
    - Stir in soy sauce and fish sauce.
4. **Serve:**
    - Garnish with fresh cilantro before serving.

Thai Sesame Chicken Wings

Ingredients:

- 1 kg chicken wings
- 2 tablespoons soy sauce
- 1 tablespoon sesame oil
- 1 tablespoon honey
- 2 cloves garlic, minced
- Sesame seeds for garnish

Instructions:

1. **Marinate Wings:**
    - In a bowl, mix soy sauce, sesame oil, honey, and garlic. Add chicken wings and marinate for at least 30 minutes.
2. **Bake:**
    - Preheat the oven to 400°F (200°C). Place wings on a baking sheet and bake for 30-35 minutes until crispy.
3. **Garnish:**
    - Sprinkle with sesame seeds before serving.

Thai Curry Puffs

Ingredients:

- 1 package puff pastry
- 1 cup cooked chicken, shredded
- 1/2 cup potatoes, diced and cooked
- 1/4 cup curry paste
- 1 egg, beaten (for egg wash)

Instructions:

1. **Prepare Filling:**
    - In a bowl, mix chicken, potatoes, and curry paste.
2. **Assemble Puffs:**
    - Roll out puff pastry and cut into circles. Place filling in the center, fold over, and seal the edges.
3. **Bake:**
    - Preheat the oven to 375°F (190°C). Brush with beaten egg and bake for 20-25 minutes until golden.
4. **Serve:**
    - Serve warm with a dipping sauce.

Thai Fried Wontons

Ingredients:

- 1 package wonton wrappers
- 200g ground pork or chicken
- 1/4 cup green onions, chopped
- 1 tablespoon soy sauce
- Oil for frying

Instructions:

1. **Prepare Filling:**
   - In a bowl, mix ground meat, green onions, and soy sauce.
2. **Fill Wontons:**
   - Place a small amount of filling in the center of each wonton wrapper. Wet the edges with water, fold, and seal.
3. **Fry Wontons:**
   - Heat oil in a pan over medium heat. Fry wontons until golden brown.
4. **Serve:**
   - Serve with sweet chili sauce.

Thai Sweet Potato and Coconut Dessert

Ingredients:

- 2 sweet potatoes, peeled and cubed
- 1 cup coconut milk
- 1/4 cup sugar
- A pinch of salt
- Sesame seeds for garnish

Instructions:

1. **Cook Sweet Potatoes:**
    - Steam or boil sweet potatoes until tender.
2. **Make Coconut Sauce:**
    - In a saucepan, heat coconut milk, sugar, and salt until dissolved.
3. **Combine:**
    - Serve sweet potatoes drizzled with coconut sauce and sprinkle with sesame seeds.

www.ingramcontent.com/pod-product-compliance
Lightning Source LLC
LaVergne TN
LVHW081505060526
838201LV00056BA/2938